Manifest

(A collection of Poems Written by Destin Howard)

Introduction:

The poems in this book are about lessons that I've learned not only about myself but the world around me. These poems and short stories discuss topics of race, religion, happiness, childhood, identity and more. To whoever may be reading this, one thing that I hope you learn is that you are in control of your destiny. That might sound cliché, but I believe that we all have the power to manifest and accomplish whatever we want, if you put in the work. This book is proof of that. Thank you for reading.

Contents

Eyes

When u look at yourself tell me what you see.

Black, Brown.

Something that resembles the color of mud and the dirt beneath the sol of my feet.

When I was little, I wanted to see a brown boy with blue eyes.

Because those eyes, well they saw everything.

Those eyes have never seen pain, only love, only privilege, grace, acceptance.

This little brown boy wants blue eyes deeper than the sea his ancestors traveled, who would never have to realize that his skin is thick.

To resist the world's lashes.

To heal generational wounds.

He won't have to see that his hair is coiled, and difficult to manage.

They tried to manage him his whole life to do things "right", or to do things white

He won't need to know.

But unfortunately, he can hear.

He can hear the slander of his race, as if somehow it puts him in second place.

Why can't people stop talking with their mouths and start and start talking with their mind

It's not that hard to be kind.

I can barely be kind to myself.

This boy looks back at himself, looking for an ounce of wealth.

Eyes turn from blue to black, and he still sees brown mud, mud that turns into clay, into stone.

 God says, "Boy don't you know are never alone."

Boy answers, "no."

Boy answers again, "but nobody here looks like me, they don't talk like me, they don't like me."

God answers, "boy they don't like what they don't understand.

Take your head outta the sand. You are a king, you are man.

They wanna be greater. They can't speak in tongues the way we do; they can't fly like we do, they wanna live the way we do. So, when they step to you, open your eyes and say

Who are you?

because I made You."

, "but…"

"I made you".

Go, Go Power Ranger

"What do you wanna be when you grow up?" Teacher asks

This was easy. I was the first one to raise my hand, and I said, "I wanna be a Power Ranger." (The blue one of course)

The Teacher asked why

Well Power Rangers can do anything; all they have do is call on their powers and things magically appear

It's kind of like speaking things into existence.

After being blown up a couple times, beat up a little bit, and maybe even thrown out 100-foot-tall robot

They always get back up.

A good ranger invites danger, disaster, defeat and even the devil.

Because the ranger knows none of his weapons will prosper, and

The best part is that they do it all with a smile

The pain only last for a little while,

and I can do it all in a slim blue suit

Third Grade

I loved the third grade.

My grades were always pretty good, but when teacher parent conferences came around, I was always a little uneasy because I talked,

A lot.

But the meeting started out well, she was saying you have a great son, in fact he does some of my job for me.

Now, This is where I got nervous.

She told them that I was telling the other people's children they going to hell.

Now at the time, I thought I was helping them out.

There was this one time this one boy that had cursed in class, and I looked at him and said

"you gone burn"

and It was probably followed by a

"Yo mama doesn't talk to you, do she?"

 Because if I did or said half of the stuff those kids did, I would have got the most fearsome ass whooping you would have ever seen. They'd say: Or maybe heard my parents say something along the lines of

Imma knock yo ass into next week,

 I am not one of your lil friends,

Get that bass out your voice

If you run away, please do not come back

See in my family we talk to each other and you if you listen, you learn some things

I learned that if I ever decide to come home past the hours of 3am my stuff will be outside.

I learned that I should never bring home a C. Because they told me that I was better than that.

I learned that I must work twice as hard as any of the other kids. Because they told me God has a plan for me.

I didn't know how to fully read until I think the second grade or third grade because apparently instead of reading, I had just memorized entire books that were read to me.

I was told that I probably should not tell people that.

But to me it shows the capacity of my mind is limitless.

Forrest Type of Friend

Get you a Forrest type of friend.

A friendship that's stupid and uncomplicated and never waited for a proper introduction.

A love that crutches can't break because your heart always aces for one another.

I said "run Forrest run" because you've already won at this game called life,

yet you run through your in zones to find me again your Lieutenant Dan.

When my legs are blown off and I'm not doing alright you say something stupid like I look so light making it a little easier for me to sleep at night.

Your honest in every single way when I ask you how you're doing say you gotta pee.

Not just because it's true but because you'd never lie to me.

You're my shield in every fight I face you beat them down without a trace.

After neglecting your love, you loved me every day.

Even in my death you said if there's anything I need you won't be far away.

I told you that you didn't know what love was and you proved me wrong.

For you it's easier than playing ping pong.

In this crazy box of chocolates that we call life you never know what you're gone get but with Forrest it's alright

So, I'll be the Jenny to your Forrest if you can be the Forrest to my Jen I'll never leave your side stay forever pass the end.
Just be my Forrest type of friend.

Dear People

Dear black people, why we dropping out?

I'm keeping my composure not to cuss you out

Dear white people,

just because we don't disperse the same intellectual aroma doesn't mean we don't deserve the same high school diploma.

Dear white people, just because I'm brown and indifferent doesn't make your imperfections any less than mine.

Dear white people, I'm not saying your all bad, I'm saying I'm jealous

That your picked first and I'm "the worst"

I'm jealous of the way you're universally accepted nor corrected.

Dear white people, I'm jealous of your privilege

Im jealous of the way your mama didn't name you the way that she named me

Not because that's the way she wanted to but because that's the way she needed too.

So somewhere somehow down the road you could get a job.

So Dear brown people,

You are beautifully and wonderfully made and don't let anyone ever tell you different.

Dear brown people, you are judged not by the color of your skin but by the content of your character.

Dear brown people, you are made for freedom

made for equality and made for a dream that we often forget.

Caffeinated Dreams

I need my coffee at midnight

In my bed so warm snuggled tight

No sugar - but hella cream.

I don't sugar code my words, so I won't sugar code these dreams.

This caffeinated metaphorically medicated magic I call art. This part of my being transpires best at my bed side. As I slide into a rush awakening.

I've awakened in my dreams.

I'm a lucid walker but a realist. My future is sweet with black bitter shots.

Not everything's meant to be smooth, sometimes u might need a lil burn on that tongue to simmer u down.

Simmer and see not everyone want what's in your cup. We want a lil flavor

Simmer and sit blow off that steam and deem yourself a blessing

Simmer down, enjoy every sip, second, and swallow. Because after all you poured it.

God provided the beans, but you ground them into perfection

The World came sour and you made it sweet.

Gave it smell that saturates defeat.

No longer will we steep in negativity

You need marinate percolate producing purer premonitions of positivity.

Powerful palates produce happiness.

This ain't your ordinary sugar rush, but an infinite high.

Now take your shot and take yo' ass to sleep.

But don't actually sleep, reap the lesson I taught you and let your mind wander deep.

Can you, lucid walk or even run, then fly can you touch the stars and see the sun go by.

But when you arise, we operate like spies

Get you a coffee keep moving by don't let no shit stop you cuz you a fly guy.

Live your best life so we can meet in the next life and keep on living.

No matter if we dead or awake we can make some shake.
You ain't gotta sit and bake for your dreams to come true

Stay Alive

Live your best life, so we can meet in the next life and keep on living.

No matter if we're dead or awake we can make some shake.
You don't have to sit and wait for your dreams to come true.

What Is Women/ Mrs. Good Women

A Women is naturally yet mentally divine They can find the things a man's eye is blind to.

Society's only breathing pacer test producing results of the oppressed men give your mouth a rest and look around you.

She may be your rib, but without her you can't stand without her what is man.

She ain't got to be your Women.

She ain't got to be your boo.

But you're going to need one or two to stand beside you because

You know Clyde wasn't shit without Bonnie

Mr. FDR was RIP long before he left the White House, he became the mouse

Michelle ran that thang showing the world we a bunch of fat orangutans, needing to expand our membranes to get what she's laying down

When my mother's sleep, I don't make a sound not because she's physically tired but because she's emotionally drained by society's bullshit.

A Woman is Strong, She's Strong where it counts.

So, She Stuff Shit up and we get mad when she screams shit out and you still wonder bout why she left you.

Where you see a whore, I see my graffiti Queen.

She's beautiful in ways that you don't understand.

I'm not talking about her thighs, hips, the sweet crescent of her lips, but the beauty of her words.

The beauty in the bread she brings home.

Beauty in the strength to stand alone.

Beauty in her intellect and art she displays.

Passion for all of my days.

That female passion that female power often mistaken for war.

Because a Woman's scorn might make the devil scream.

A good woman's very nature like a stream should provide direction.

A good woman is kind to blind because they know not what they've done.

A good woman is one who sits on her throne with compassion.

A good woman is one that knows how to ration out her love.

Because us good men can't always do that because not all of us were taught how.

A Women can be sun in your storm or the lighting that blazes your fires

She's the call you put on mute but still reminds you with a voicemail

You're the worm and she's that early bird that set you free.

Because she knows better than anyone what it means to have your hopes, your dreams swallowed and broken.

A woman is many things but a good Woman
Ms. Good woman knows the right way to love.

Thank, Miss Rona

Dear, Miss Rona (COVID 19),

You ruined my birthday

I was supposed to be on the beach - but Noooo.

You felt the need to confiscate all of outside to yourself.

You decided that it would be a good idea for me to take 18 hours' worth of classes online.

You made me find a new appreciation for stay at home moms. Because I couldn't handle that.

You gave me back my family

You brought me back to an internal infinity of interstellar space.

If it weren't for you, I wouldn't have written this book.

I would've never breathed the cleanest air that these lungs have swallowed in years,

never pumped blood as rich as gold,

never found my center.

You've taken a lot,

but not from me.

The only thing you took from me was structure.

This was mostly academic.

Don't get me wrong, you stressed me out sometimes.

But I'm not mad at you,

Anymore.

So, thank you for the gift, but

you've overstayed your welcome.

\\

.

FAITH

Most people's faith is the size of a mustard seed.

Yet you wonder why you can't walk on water,

why your trees bear no fruit.

Did you start at the root?

Plant joyful seeds like groot.

When I was in the 5th grade my dad got shot.

Months go by, he bounced back just fine he walked a straight line, but my brother went narrow.

Got sentenced to 3 and a half years they dropped to 2

They will drop to 1, he will come home soon.

You have to claim things.

Ask and you shall receive.

So, stop asking for things that you can measure.

Is it that hard for you to see Him in yourself?

Is it that hard for you to trust anybody else?

Where is your faith?

In Him,

In yourself?

Don't you want to fall abundantly into your healing, into your health?

This should be easy because we are divinely blessed and highly favored

I am divinely blessed and highly favored.

PSA

This a letter to let you know what I write about

I've been told I have eagle like talons,

been told I have eagle like claws, flaws beyond comparison.

But what about these eagles like wings, these eagle eyes, this wise mentality to kind to make a comeback,

yet too smart for that sappy shit, but I love that sappy shit no need for a clap back.

You'll never see me cry

You'll never see me sigh

You might just see me fly

I wanna see you fly

Do you ever see me die as I do every day?

Mirror says aye I'm reinforcing your dysphoria, can I have your heart and I'll surely make sure that you feel pain and I told it yes.

These are the things that I write about, that I might lie to your face about, the things that I cry about when u leave the room.

But it's not all bad

I start in the whole so I can dig myself-out I don't talk too loud so u can figure out

I remember the past, so I know where I'm going.

I'm built like a tree that means I'm still growing

Ja said water your seeds because nothing blooms all year.

If u don't work on your harvest, you'll surely disappear

Listen to the great vine branches on this tree.

Maybe you can learn something and teach it back to me.

You see it's not all bad but it sure as hell ain't good.

As far as I'm concerned, I'm still in my childhood

Living my best life licking lollipops losing teeth that eventually grow back.

Falling on the playground and I get back up

Get home with rocks in my shoes so I throw them up

The bully comes around, so I lift him up

 to God

God won't give us nothing we can't handle you were built for this

You just gotta recognize your mantle.

I'm That Melanie magic, That Black and Bold, This ivory Gold.

Yeah, we mess up here and we mess up there but,

I love myself so I really don't care

This isn't an explanation it's a PSA

So, you should probably listen to things I say.

Poetry Poem

I know these words don't have to rhyme.

But when I think about its hard not to make it align and rhyme, and match in time.

So, it can maybe touch a heart and make it melt, like slime.

But I don't write for other people.

I can't write per request.

I write per self-necessity.

So, when I feel less than me, I'm reminded I can fly.

I'm reminded that I can fly or be fly far from florescent fears of humanity's reach.

Where I can mentally reteach,

My mind to relook, research and find something better about myself.

When I write I do so silently, but the words are the loudest in the room.

I get consumed in everything and nothing at all.

Nothing matters at all but the way you feel.

Are you happy?

Are you glad?

Like the heavy weight trash bag?

Is that smile on your face a cover up for how sad your existence really is?

This is something that can't be defined, but only felt.

This is pain.

This is love.

This is every dream you've dreamt of dreaming of.

So, what is poetry?

When you figure it out let me know?

Please Don't Buy Me Roses

If u really want to get my attention you should buy me flowers.

But Please Don't by me roses.

Because by now we should all know that they have thorns.

But when I saw you all I saw was a dying bloom

And a pot that left little room

for any other seeds but I planted one anyway.

But this plant this rose was actually more of a Venus fly trap,

That bit my head off at a moment's notice.

I planted my happiness.

I planted my forgiveness.

You let me waste, I mean plant my time into you.

But that's my fault.

I should've dug you up before I let you move in; I mean settle in the ground with me.

I would've saw that your roots were already dead.

I thought that you just never wanted to grow with me.

Turns out you actually couldn't.

Nor did you want to, but that's beside the point.

Now we're here in this mess of a pot.

This messy pot.

With me this Tall, Tenacious, Talented, Sexy ass, Tulip.

And you,

this bloom

that was actually a withered down rose without any more thorns to fight with.

So, when you cheated, I wasn't mad

I was just tired of pulling up your weeds.

So, to the next pot that feels the need to be planted.

I like flowers, I really do
I just don't like roses anymore.

February 14ᵗʰ

Today Started off as a normal day surrounded by my friends this artificial family that loves me

You see, we lived, loved, leaned on one another as if you were my blood brother, boy.

I guess you might as well be

She placed a candy in my hand, I said thank you my friend, yet I still feel empty

The day was going on just fine, another twisted my hair with every tender pull my heart felt pain

The pull of my heart when you left without return when I was discerned about what you left behind, I called and said it was your paper when I really wanted to say me.

You left me

You all left me alone as I've always been.

I know I said forget love, but I'm lonely.

I want someone.

I want someone like that someone that wants you.

I want someone like that someone that asked you out.

I want someone like that someone that asked me about you.

I want someone to want.

Me too

I want someone to look at me and say they love me and,

I know yall love me but yall know it's not the same so from here where do I go?

Someone tell me from here where I should go? because I honestly don't know.

I know I don't wanna die alone as I've always known I would.

That's why in the future I ask to baby sit your kids because I know I'll never have any of my own, I mean I don't want any of my own because know of days kids wanna act grown but at least I can ensure yours find love.

After yall left I didn't call until the move because I didn't wanna cock block I didn't wanna knock knock on something important.

After or if I ever let you hear this don't feel pitty keep smiling with your kitty keep it litty like a titty lift your spirts up or even bust down whatever you do keep your head of above the ground because at least you got someone.

Someone to want you,

Happy valentine's day 2019

My Locs

Do you like my baby locs.

My hair the way we are.

 I think I'm finally out of that ugly stage.

That you look in the mirror and say, "Damn Nigga you ugly" stage.

That shrinking stage, when no matter what you do, you find yourself smaller.

I was once told, you'll never see a nice man with dreadlocks.

I was once told, you'll never get a good job with dreadlocks.

Well 1st of all, I don't want a job.

I want a career.

My locs will be so long, so famous, you'll know my name from ear to ear.

My locs will be so strong, you can never break us off. I'm not a knock off.

My locs will be so long my shadow has to run to catch up with me.

My locs will be so long that the tips touch the ground.

But they never drag.

They never drag things behind, because that would be dreadful wouldn't it.

I don't dread anything I do.

My locs will be unbound,

unafraid,

heavenly made.

My locs will be so long that they can whip anyone that ever doubted me.

My locs will be long enough to reach out and wrap around the necks of anyone

That ever called me nigga,

Anyone that ever called me boy, &

Anyone that ever chose not to believe in me.

My locs are divinely blessed and highly favored

My locs represent greatness

As will I.

Self-Made Millionaires

When I become a millionaire.

I wonder if I will be satisfied.

When I become a millionaire,

I wonder if I will be happy.

Who wouldn't be, except me?

I think I'll be happy when I have my dad get his boat.

I will be happy when my mom's latest home makeover idea comes true.

People say money can't buy happiness but let's be honest,

It does.

Because I don't know about you, but imma be really happy when God blesses me with that rent.

No, actually I'll be happy with that mortgage.

 I even start dancing when I get my first car note.

You know, I'll never understand why people get so mad at bills.

Like, people start talking to it like the bill did something wrong.

I'm sorry that you wanted water.

I'm sorry that you wanted shelter.

I'm sorry that you thought it would be a good idea to invest in something that you weren't ready for.

Sometimes you have to work, wait, scream, cry, but most of all be patient.

There are no self-made Millionaires,

and I know that the word has 3 I's in it but none of them stand for I

The 1st stands for I am, the most, high father Jesus Christ

The 2nd invests in me. and

The 3rd, infinity, because unlike money, God last forever.

There are no self-made Millionaires

 it usually takes 3 people the CEO, the trinity

but there are partnerships

he'll give you a gift in exchange for an indefinite loan of faith.

When I become a millionaire, I'll be in a lot of debt

But at least I only owe one person.

Who is James?

Do you know me, or do you know James?

Don't get me wrong, Destin is a pretty cool guy, but James, is that nigga

Destin likes to go outside, run, do a little poetry, and James does too, but there's some differences

Like how Destin has 1 speeding ticket and James has a been pulled over more than 5 times, has had 1 speeding ticket, and lost track of the number of parking violations.

Another one is how, for instance I have never drank alcohol a day in my life

James however likes to drink

A lot

James likes to drink so much that one time he got an orgasm just thinking about it. James can take up to about 12 shots of tequila on a good day. However, Destin would probably throw up after like 2.

But both of us do like to party it's just that I'm back at 12 and James comes back by 3…. Sometimes.

James also may have sort of, kind of, maybe used to have been a little bit of a hoe. But not anymore, he's changed his ways he's doing better and settling down. But I wouldn't have the slightest idea of what a warm body feels like.

But James he gets what he wants

James doesn't have a filter

He doesn't have to be polite to everyone, nor does he ever doubt himself, He is fearless

He had a boyfriend

I think it's time that me and James came together

I think it's time that we became one.

Funeral Plans

Don't cry at my funeral.

If you do only let it last a little while.

Because in that moment I guarantee I won't be thinking of you.

I'll be hitting the two step, cha cha slide, I glide into the light that is holy.

So please don't cry.

Be happy I made it. Be happy I'm home.

The streets are brighter than Dorothy's yellow brick road

He paints me in gold and I'm worth every ounce.

Nothing amounts to paradise.

Why would we waist tears on a corpse.

I ran my course and I ran it well, after all someone has to stay and tell the tale.

Don't wait till I'm casket sharp to say you miss me because I'm sharp every day.

Instead of over obsessing omnipotent obituaries transcribe my talents through the tongue.

But please don't cry.

Throw me a party

American Lies

This week I heard a white man say

"All they wanna do is be ghetto"

Last week I saw I headline saying

"Studies show that cops kill more white citizens that black"

Today, a white woman at the polls screamed "This is America"

This is America

A place where ghetto is more than a place of residents, but a characteristic

A place where media outlets are too dumb to realize that black people only make up 13% of the population.

This is America where we love to tell lies, like All lives matter.

This is America where survival is a white man's birth right, and black man's greatest achievement.

This is America

To the white woman impatient at the polls. You have waited for 12 hours

Try waiting for 400 years get told no, you're a woman, wait 50 more an get back to me

My favorite lie is this is America land of the free and home of the brave.

I'm only brave because I have to be

here in America where the 6 o'clock news sounds like a horror film.

The only monsters I see bare blue eyes and bullets.

I daydream your American nightmare.

If only Michael knew this is America where skittles are reserved for satins sustenance.

If only Ahmuad knew running was still a threat to their authority.

If only Breonna knew to never close her eyes, to never sleep. Because it might be the last time you open them.

This America where we tell lies, like make America great again,

To me that sounds a lot like a death sentence.

America where "When the looting starts the shooting starts" because to you my life isn't worth a pair of Nike shoes and Gucci belt.

 You call this violent behavior

Well you taught us violence.

You even taught a class last week shooting rubber bullets, disrupting the peace for a photo op

You say do not burn down your homes.

What home?

We own nothing.

My people, our people built this for yours.

Or did you forget, this is America

Land of the wicked and home of the horrified.

Realizations

realized that there is nothing bliss about your ignorance

realized that bliss is temporary you'll see they'll never love you if last forever maybe that's why I hear silent smiles every time you bleed out.

realized that they have never stopped aiming at this brown colored bullseye I call flesh. Instead hey went from arrows to a rope. From a rope to a water hose, from a water hose to a gun.

remembered that the winners of wars write history.

guess you went and called yourself the Avatar no wonder my blood bends when I think of

Eric, Sandra, George, Ahmuad.

Or maybe you called Scar you have endangered us kings and lioness.

I have seen too many Mufasa's in the sky

Or maybe you went and called yourself God.

You made me a scarecrow even named me Jimmy, and I silently smile as you taught me to do Oh so well.

I've realized people only build scarecrows when they're afraid.

I've realized the easiest way to make headlines is to make my blood grey.

White on black, because black on black crime is a normal abnormalcy.

There is nothing normal about premature mortality. There is nothing normal about mass incarceration.

But yet you smile

Sunday after Sunday in sweet sanctuary serenaded by sorrow with a scenery of society

But yet you smile Oh so silently.

I realized maybe your god never taught you to speak.

But my god.

Taught me to do all things, I start with the small things and grow to fruition.

Give your smile purpose and unstitch your cries

I realized I'm the reason god says nigga for the first time.

He'll say, "Got damn nigga you've done a job well done."

The End

(Thanks for reading)